Empowered to Win

Overcoming the Impossible

Kimberly Glover

EMPOWERED TO WIN- Overcoming the Impossible.

Please direct all copyright inquiries to:
B.O.Y. Enterprises, Inc.
c/o Author Copyrights
P.O. Box 262
Lowell, NC 28098

Paperback ISBN: 978-1-955605-39-7

Cover and Interior Design: B.O.Y. Enterprises, Inc.

Author Photos: Cierra Moore

Printed in the United States.

Table of Contents

Chapter 1

Peer Pressure

Growing up, everyone imagines their lives evolving in a specific way. Some would call it the perfect life, while others call it their dream life. Throughout our entire academic career, teachers and counselor are preparing students for college. What will you do in the real world some might ask? Are you going to college, or will you get a job? We spend our entire childhood learning and preparing for adulthood. Society teaches us to prepare our children for the future before birth. This type of pressure can cause parents to experience anxiety, and some sort of frustration early on. While others may experience joy and determination to have their child take on the family business.

In every culture, there are different practices set in place with one common goal, to raise a successful child into becoming a successful adult. I have discovered throughout the years that successful living is intentional. Even when we are given the necessary tools to achieve success, we must intentionally choose to walk in it.

I call heaven and earth to record this day against you, that I have set before you life and death, blessings and cursing: therefore, choose life that both thou and thy seed may live." -**Deuteronomy 30:19 KJV**

One of the most pivotal points in a child's life is in their adolescent years. This stage of life can be described as a shaping point. During this stage of life, many teenagers are determining their future endeavors. Which pathway will I take is the big question? Do I follow the crowd that leads to popularity, which is full of peer pressure? Do I follow my parent's road map to success, or do I, in this season discover the God ordained plan for my life and walk in it? Remember that the choice is yours!

Transitioning from middle school to high school can be challenging, however success is a choice! Movies, music videos, entertainment, books, and our environment all are noise pollution aiming to cloud our very judgment of life. I call these things not only noise pollution, and distractions, but image falsification. My personal definition of image falsification is a misrepresentation of a modeled picture of perfection.

There are no perfect or exact ways to achieve success. However, there are some pathway models available to point us all in a direction that may equip us for a certain level of success. For instance, attending a trade school, a four-year university, having an internship, and studying can have a positive effect on success. On the reverse side, becoming a lazy person with no knowledge of a company, acquiring no skills will guarantee failure. Hosea 4:6 says that my people are destroyed because of a lack of knowledge.

There is a distinct separation between the "smart kids", and the kids that just skate through high school. Which category will you fit into? As a freshman in high school, I already knew which category I wanted to fit into. By default, I was considered one of the popular students. I came into high school as a cheerleader, and because of that, a lot of people knew my name. Cheerleaders, football players, basketball player, and anyone who played a sport were all considered jocks, the so-called popular kids.

When entering high school, I already had a best friend. I knew my teammates because of summer cheer practice. When the school year began, I became acclimated with my classes and adjusted well to high school. Like other teenagers, I already laid out my plans which included a list of dos and don'ts.

One of the things that I did not want initially in high school was a boyfriend. My friends and I all made a pact that we would hold on to our virginity, and that we would not become boy crazy. My philosophy was that boys brought on trouble, and I did not want any distractions. It is funny how a few months can change one's philosophy. The very thing that I despised was the very thing that I was drawn to. I figured if I avoided dating, then I could avoid the kind of trouble that I was not ready for.

Freshmen year went extremely well other than the fact that I had to attend summer school. During summer school, I met a lot of people from different local high schools in the DC area. Summer school placement in DC, was based on the ward that you attended school in during the normal academic year. My new friends and I made a small bet about who could earn the highest-grade point average by the end of the summer. I won of course earning a 4.0 which in turn prompted me to continue earning good grades throughout my high school tenure. This was the summer that my life took a huge turn.

I broke the pack that my friends and I made. I found out that one of the other freshman boys was crushing on me and wanted to be my boyfriend. I did not know too much about having a boyfriend, but I thought that he was a nice guy, so I accepted the offer. In my mind, I thought that this new boyfriend would just be a summer crush, but our relationship went well into the following school year. This relationship lasted throughout my freshmen year in college. My friends were very accepting of my new relationship, they welcomed him into our circle with open arms.

As I began to introduce my new boyfriend to everyone that was important to me, no one seemed to object to this new relationship. My plans were to keep this relationship pure; I was not even comfortable in the beginning with the thought of touching at all. Remember I was the one who came up with the no boyfriend idea in the beginning. As the months passed, my boyfriend and I grew closer, remaining pure. We did not engage in anything more than a hug and maybe holding hands occasionally.

After six months of the relationship, we began to kiss more so with hellos and goodbyes. I was new at this relationship thing! Looking back at this relationship, I believe that we were very immature. What started off as something so innocent became something that would change our lives forever. Innocent per Merriam webster is defined as lacking or reflecting a lack of sophistication, guile, or self-consciousness: Alertness, Ingenuous).

Before I accepted the offer to become his girlfriend, I set boundaries in place. Some of the boundaries included a verbal list of dos and don'ts. We went on this relationship journey in full expectations of having a long-term plan for the future. Honestly, looking back at the conversations that we had as teenagers, you would have thought that we were laying out a contract for marriage. As I dive deeper into this book, I will change up some of the characters names to protect their identities. For the purpose of this book, I will call my former boyfriend Jacob.

Jacob and I began to spend all our free moments together. Whether it was walking through the halls together or meeting up for lunch, we made time for each other. In the beginning, we did not take classes together, however by the time that we entered our junior year of high school, we took most of our classes together. Re-thinking about how it was in the beginning, we were experiencing what teenagers call puppy love. I define puppy love as a false sense of true love, this love is typically experienced in adolescent years when one or two people become infatuated with the other.

In today's spiritual terminology, we were entangled in a soul tie. There are different types of soul ties that people can experience, it really depends on the depth of the relationship that has been formed. It was apparent that we were learning how to depend completely on each other, little did we know that were heading down a road that leads to destruction.

The type of destruction I am referring to is destruction of a friendship. This type of destruction usually leads married couples to divorce court. Here it was, our innocent high school relationship was about to take a turn for the worst and neither one of us were ready for this. How many people can honestly admit that they, at one time or another, allowed other people to influence their relationship decision? Often, other people will give you advice that they themselves will never take. These types of people are called intruders!

Intruders have a lot to say and love to come in between other people's relationships. Intruders can come in the form of family members and close friends. Intruders sometimes start off meaning well in their advice, and they usually were once invited into intimate conversations with one or both parties involved in the relationship. In the beginning this person can be viewed as neutral with the intentions of helping one or both persons in the relationship to resolve a challenge. After a while, the person become invasive, offering up their opinion concerning a situation that no one solicited their opinion for. Suddenly, the invasiveness becomes pushy and aggressive.

What was once helpful, has now become a hinderance, and instead of one or both of you addressing the issue, you allow the behavior to continue inviting an unwanted intruder to call shots in your relationship. Jacob and I were allowing people outside of relationship to carry weight in our decision making. This is extremely dangerous and is a form of not only invasiveness by intruders, but also a form of peer pressure!

At the two-year mark of our relationship peer pressure began to give us advice. One never really hears of peer pressure bringing about positive results. I believe that peer pressure is a voice with a hidden agenda. Peer pressure's agenda is to get a person to agree with a false or artificial reality. When you think about where peer pressure is derived from, it typically comes from your peers in a social group.

As teenagers we tend to hold our friends to higher standard as if they were family. During this season of our lives, what our friends thought about us truly mattered. The danger in soliciting advice or receiving unwanted advice can come without a warning sign. Warning signs are just that, it warns you about an eminent threat.

Warning signs trigger signals to the brain to fight or flight. What happens when the warning signs are being ignored because the people who are opposing an immediate threat are those who are in your inner circle? In this case it would take a greater level of maturity and intentionality to stand firm on your core values and beliefs. Sometimes a warning sign can be trigger based on the words that someone speaks to you, or even from some personal suggestions concerning a specific matter. Either way, it is important to understand warning signs and their triggers no matter where they come from. Always remain on high alert!

Back to peer pressure, the method of operation is to cause someone to break all the rules and morals that they have concerning a specific area of their life and go against it. Peer pressure can disguise itself as a voice of reason and or wisdom. Once you take the bait of peer pressure, its friend reason begins to enter your heart as well. Reason is the "should I do this or that" complex.

Reason suggests that you will not really lose your values and principles in life for going against your prior expectation of yourself. Reason encourages you to think about the possibility of nothing bad happening for changing your mind. Reason is designed to justify your actions mentally even before physically acting on it. Reason tells your mind that she is wisdom. Let me interject here for a moment! Reason and wisdom are not the same thing!

For my boyfriend and I, the voice of peer pressure was telling us to have sex although we were not ready to make any adult permanent decisions. Reasoning began to enter our relationship. The thought of suggestion to engage in sexual relations produced reasoning of why we should, that was not present before peer pressure entered. My boyfriend's homeboys were telling him that he was whipped, saying things like, your girlfriend has you wrapped around her finger and on top of that, she is not even giving it up.

You see, the voice of peer pressure gets louder and louder if you do not tell it to shut up at the onset. Instead of my boyfriend telling peer pressure to shut up, he yielded to the voice of peer pressure, and now the idea of engaging in sexual intercourse was a part of our conversations. We began to include reasoning into our conversation, making every excuse of why we should engage in sexual intercourse, saying things like, it is time for us to take our relationship to the next level. We even said that engaging in sexual intercourse would allow us to express our love for each other. That in fact was the number one lie that we told each other and agreed on!

The Bible tells us that God is love, and love gives! Here we were in our teenage mindsets attempting to define a love that neither one of us truly knew. That is the number one trick of the enemy, sex is not an expression of love when you are single. Sex was designed for married people only, an outward expression of the two becoming one through consummation of their covenant. The idea of engaging in sexual intercourse should be an adult decision that comes with adult consequences. Ladies and gentlemen please stop falling for the, I love you syndrome, then giving into temptation which ultimately produces feelings, emotions, and suggestions that are not truly present. Let us be honest right quick, it is the lust of the flesh from a feeling of infatuation that get us caught up many times. We tend to say things like this; he or she gives me butterflies! Why do we use a temporary feeling to describe an emotion that we are currently experiencing to make life altering decisions?

Let me take a minute to really define love. God is love, and until you first receive the love of God you do not know what love is. Love is not an emotion that is felt. I can boldly proclaim this because, how are we fall able madly in love with a person, then after we have some sort of disagree or altercation, we no longer love or respect the person when a breakup is involved? This is because we were infatuated with the person, or the idea of having that type of relationship. God is love! **John 3:16 NLT**, *"For this is how God loved the world: He gave his one and only Son, so that everyone who believes in him will not perish but have eternal life."*

Love is a decision; a choice, and the true God kind of love is not based on a feeling. The true Agape love is unconditional. Unconditional love says that I will love you in the good and bad times. Marriages are built on the very foundation of unconditional love, henceforth when a vow or oath is made before God, both parties agree to the statement; for richer or poorer, in sickness and in health as long as both shall live. We understand that there are rules to be adhered to in this type of covenant or there are consequences that one will face.

We often fall victim to the words I love you. As a teenager, I just wanted to be loved! Honestly ask yourself this question, what type of love are you looking for? I was looking for love in all the wrong places. This time I was caught up in a false reality, I had given myself in to the lust of the flesh. Today, I understand that what we meditate on becomes our reality, and sometimes our reality and what the current facts are may seem to contradict one another. No child should take any solicited or unsolicited advice from other children when it comes to extremely sensitive subject matters.

Society has made it extremely uncomfortable for adolescent to talk about sexual intercourse with their parents and or another trusted adult. Sexual intercourse is one of those subject matters that comes with many thoughts, ideas, and suggestions. People of all ages both young and mature mistake sexual intercourse as an act to express their love for one another outside of the marriage bed.

The expression of love can take up many different forms without the presence of sexual intercourse. To the young mindset, it is common to hear a couple state that they are in love and have decided to take their relationship to the next level. Society has created and normalized this notion that sex outside of marriage is great way to express one's emotional feelings to another. What society has failed to explain is that sexual intimacy performed prematurely not only comes with physical consequences (pregnancy, and STI's), it may also come with emotional pain.

Emotional pain is pain that is caused by a non-physical source, meaning that it is derived from some sort of mental trauma. It is the type of pain that only God can heal you of. People often turn to prayer; some may seek counseling when they themselves are unable to handle or become free of this type of pain on their own. What they did not tell me is that the moment I chose to make an adult decision like this one, that I would be in for a whirlwind of negative emotions. The negative emotions that I experienced caused me so much emotional trauma and pain. Nevertheless, the decision was made!

We decided to engage in sexual intercourse. Parents, teenagers, young adults, please be sure to make an inform decision before engaging in life altering behaviors. Many times, we may have great intentions for the actions that we chose to engage in without being fully informed on the possible outcomes. Let us take a moment and think about why we feel the need to rush into sexual intercourse, or sexual intimacy. Were we really ready for this type of change in dynamics with that person, if we are honest with ourselves? Honestly, we need to take a moment and seek some wise counsel, understand the consequences, and identify some triggers as to why we as teenagers and young adults are haphazardly making these choices to jump into bed with someone who we are not in covenant with.

The truth is that we have allowed a moment in time to justify the decisions that we make and the actions that we take! Nevertheless, although I knew internally that this choice would ultimately change the trajectory of our relationship, I agreed to move forward. If we can be honest again about the decisions that we are making, it comes from taking the thought, meditating on the action while allowing it to become a desire. If we really did not want to make that type of decision, then we would have just used our door of escape. When we are in Christ Jesus, He will always give us a door of escape.

What does the door of escape look like you ask? The door of escape looks like that still small voice telling you not to make that decision. In addition, that door of escape may be a feeling of apprehensiveness, it may be something that is blocking the situation from occurring. God will literally give you the answer while allowing you to make your own choices. In the end, we made the decision to engage in premarital sex! The heat was on!

Chapter 2

The Heat is On

I knew that we were not ready for sexual intercourse, but the idea of losing my boyfriend who I was so in love with came to mind. He never gave me an ultimatum of breaking up with me if I was opposed to sexual intimacy, but I was just totally confused. Remember, I myself was listening to the voice of peer pressure. Sex is an adult decision that comes with adult consequences, and if you are not ready for those consequences then you need to shut that voice up. The idea of having sex terrified me at first, and then I begin to take the suggestion of becoming intimate with my boyfriend.

It started off as something we called dry sex. Dry sex is more so foreplay with your clothes on. We did not know what we were getting ourselves into in the beginning because we could have stopped engaging in the foreplay. At this point in our relationship lust had entered our hearts.

Lust was the spiritual force that was guiding us, disguising itself as love.

I know that you are asking yourself, how do you know the difference between love and lust? Love is unconditional, it is not a feeling, it is not based on an emotion. Lust however is based on feelings, emotions, the now. Lust takes on the identity of love until the flesh is gratified. Lust acts as if its unconditional love for the other person until a situation arises. This situation can be as minor as an argument. When a situation opposes the desire of lust, then that lust will expose its true identity.

Think about it! Have you ever wondered why that boyfriend or girlfriend that you have shared all your dreams, hopes, aspirations, and fears with suddenly exposed your secrets in the heat of an argument? Take a pause moment, and again think about it! This is an indicator that he/she does not genuinely love you. The truth is, they are in lust with you!

As people we are truly relational beings. We get attached to others based on our similarities, agreements, traumas, experiences, habits, and behavior patterns. Essentially, attractions can be formed due to the same commonalities. If we were to really take a quick snapshot of the relationships and associations that we have with others, look for the common denominator. Was that relationship formed for purposes of networking, growth strategies, good intentions, or was the basis of that relationship due to a common shared experience that was rooted in hurt, anger, complaining, or bitterness?

In addition, we tend to form relationships out of the need to fulfill some type of desire or to fill a void. Looking back to that time in my life, that relationship caused me to really examine the matters of my heart in my adulthood. Getting back to the initial question of why is it that in the heat of an argument your boyfriend or girlfriend decides to use that moment to repeat a secret that you have told them, or sometimes even bring up a situation that can trigger feelings of hurt? Those types of behaviors can bring to surface the true foundation of the relationship. Was the relationship's foundation genuinely love, or was it lust?

For me, lust was exposed when our "innocent" relationship became sex driven. After we engaged in sexual intercourse it seemed as if sex became an important part of our relationship! Again, I would go back and tell my teenage self that sex is an adult decision that should be taken seriously and only engaged in within the confinement of the marriage covenant. The gifts slowly stopped, the sweet notes in my locker stopped. It began to feel like he now viewed me in a way as if I had nothing else to offer him! Remember that this is my perspective! I had given him the most precious gift that was meant to be reserved for my husband. Lust made its appearance and was definitely running and ruining our relationship!

Looking back on it today, I believe that God was providing us with many doors of escape. 1 Corinthians

10:13 NLT, *"The temptations in your life are no different from what others experience. And God is faithful. He will not allow the temptation to be more than you can stand. When you are tempted, he will show you a way out so that you can endure."*

Peer pressure presented itself once again and this time it started talking even louder. We were ok with the idea of dry sex because it came with clothes on and no penetration. Then one day our friends asked us if we were having sex, and we admitted to them that we were not having sex. It was like we were seeking approval about our sexual relationship from our friends. Why were we looking for validation from outside sources? This was definitely the breeding ground for intruders.

Beware of intruders in your relationship! Sometimes people do not know that they are in fact intruders. So, our friends started to give us a heads up about opportunities to skip school and attempt to have sex. The first time that we made the attempt to engage in sex was weird, I did not like it at all. Instead of running away right then, I stayed.

Ladies and gentlemen, God will always give you a way of escape. This was actually my second opportunity to escape this situation altogether. I was so naïve; I made my decision and chose to continue in the act. Now we were all in, and okay with the idea of having sex, so we tried it again during the morning of homecoming festivities during our junior year of High School. After engaging in sex, we went to school because I had to perform during our pep rally. Immediately, my cheer coach looked at me and knew that I gave my innocence away. I was so embarrassed, and after I got off the stage, I told my cheer sisters what I just did. My life changed forever in a moment's time.

Now that we had engaged in sexual intimacy, our relationship took a huge turn. I was no longer getting as much gifts as I was getting prior to sex, and Valentine's Day was no longer the same. Our relationship was now focused on a sexual relationship. During our senior year of high school, it happened. Skipping school or going to school late to have sex became our norm. One day we skipped school again to have sex and this time the condom broke. You often hear about stories that people make up about their girlfriend getting pregnant because of the condom breaking, but that was our true reality. The condom did break, and the evidence was growing on the inside of me.

Not only did the torn piece of condom come out of me, but my menstrual cycle was late. I began to panic. Here I was at the height of my academic career facing pregnancy. I had recently got accepted into every college that I applied to, and I had also just learned how to tumble. I was a hardcore Brainiac cheerleader. The only thing that consumed my thoughts were that I could not be pregnant, however my teenage body was showing signs of motherhood that I was not ready for!

Are you hiding anything was the only thing that I was hearing from my peers and teachers? During my senior year of high school, I was a cheer captain, JROTC queen, the Key Club President and a part of a host of other clubs.

I did not have time to be pregnant! How could that become my reality? That was not a part of my plan. I could not ignore the evidence of that huge secret that I was attempting to hide. One day I was cheering at a basketball game, and I ran offline to throw up. Not able to escape my cheer coach eyes, she knew that I was pregnant. Admitting that I was pregnant was extremely hard to do.

The next thing I knew was that I was facing the reality that my pregnancy was not going to go away. Although I had not formally taken a pregnancy test, I had not seen my menstrual cycle in approximately two months. So, my cheer sisters and other friends supported me as I went to the pregnancy care center to take my first pregnancy test. I already knew the answer before the results were told to me. The evidence was clear; my baby was growing at a rapid pace. My tight body, firm abs was beginning to expand. My size 3 and 5 clothing were too small, and my belly button was beginning to make an appearance. What am I going to do now?! Who can I safely run to in a time of trouble?

Hebrews 4:16 NKJV states, *"let us therefore come boldly unto the throne of grace that we may obtain mercy, and find grace to help in time of need."* If only then I knew what I know today about the love of God. I would have made a different decision outside of fear. This was the hardest decision of my life! How can someone who was viewed as Miss Perfect become pregnant? Would I be able to go to school every day and face my newfound reality? What this really happening to me? My thoughts were endless. I was pregnant and scared! I had now entered into the valley of decisions, a mental place that I was not ready to experience!

Chapter 3

The Valley of Decisions

Do I keep my baby, or do I abort my baby? Just the thought of aborting my baby today breaks my heart. I was 10 weeks pregnant when I officially found out. My baby was growing and my size 5 cheerleading uniform that I had worn for 4 years was becoming too small. I could no longer hide my pregnancy.

The news was spreading fast around the school and fear had made a huge appearance. You better not keep that baby is all I heard! You will ruin your life forever! What are you going to do with a baby? Where will you live? Your parents are not going to take care of you! You need to go to college and have a baby later in life! Your future is so bright and having a baby will only stop your plans! Get an abortion and go to college!

During this time, I experienced a heightened level of fear. The type of fear that causes you to make unsound decisions based on other people opinion of you. Google defines fear as an unpleasant emotion caused by the belief that someone or something is dangerous, likely to cause pain, or a threat. Merriam-Webster dictionary defines fear as to be afraid of (something or someone); to expect or worry about (something bad or unpleasant). What was I so fearful of? It was the opinions of other people. My mother esteemed me high because of my accolades, my future was very bright. Even still, I found a new love, growing on the inside of me. How could I give this up? We were one, my unborn baby and I, and I could feel every movement on the inside of me. This was not fair!

Lord please send at least one person that would support a 17-year-old mother to be. I needed a true friend. Proverbs 18:24 states, *"A man that hath friends must shew himself friendly: and there is a friend that sticketh closer than a brother. His name is Jesus!"* I did not have a relationship with Jesus at the time, so I was unaware of His friendship and support. Although I grew up in church, attending Sunday school, and bible study, if I could be honest with myself, I really did not know Jesus. I was facing a life changing decision without any support!

Disclaimer, please do not ignore the red flags and warning signs as I did! "My mother is going to put me out of the house if we tell her that you are pregnant," is what my boyfriend told me. It was at that very moment when he uttered those words that I knew I was alone in this situation. That type of reply was not only selfish, but it was devastating to me. Girl, if your boyfriend tells you something that implies that you are in a situation alone, please believe him. Remember the words that was told to me in the beginning of introducing sexual intercourse into our relationship? You probably would not remember the "I love you," let us take our relationship to the next level because at that very moment I did not feel loved.

There was nowhere for me to turn! I was pregnant and scared! Who will you turn to in a time of trouble? So, after all the pressure to have sex, I got pregnant at the age of 17 years old. Let me tell you, the pressure did not end there. Be careful of what doors you open in your life. Genesis 4:7 NKJV reads, *"If thou doest well, shalt thou not be accepted? And if thou doest not well, sin lieth at the door. And unto thee shall be his desire, and thou shall rule over him."* This scripture was completely evident in my life. I was accepted as long as I was the brainiac cheerleader whose future was bright. In the face of a life altering challenge, I was shunned.

Romans 6:23 NKJV says, *"For the wages of sin is death; but the gift of God is eternal life through Jesus Christ our Lord."* For me, I was walking in the death that this scripture speaks of. This type of death was spiritual at the time, I was left alone with my own thoughts and nowhere to turn so I thought. My sin had given rise to a premature pregnancy that everyone wanted me to end. I felt dead on the inside! I was crying out for support, and no one was listening to me. The pressure was on, and the voice was even louder than before. This time fear and peer pressure teamed up and screamed abortion.

How could I abort my baby? How could abortion be an option in anyone's mind? The hidden joy that I was experiencing at night with my unborn baby was not worth abortion. During the day, the pressure was on. Adults were offering to help me pay for the abortion and hide it from my parents. I now understand what it is like to be in a state of confusion.

I made several appointments to the abortion clinic. I had so much support when it came to aborting my baby during the weekdays and hardly any on the weekends. The day had finally come when I was going to abort my baby, but I was too afraid to go to the clinic. Another week had gone by, and I was terrified, in search of support to keep my baby. No one agreed with my decision to keep my baby.

On the next opportunity to abort my baby, my friend and I walked for hours to the abortion clinic in which today I believe that God was giving me a way of escape from. We finally reached the clinic, once inside they show you exactly how they were going to perform the abortion. It was horrific to me! I ran out of the clinic in tears explaining to my friend what was about to take place if I committed to this. I then called every adult in my phone book looking for support, and they all encouraged me to continue with the abortion. I was alone, so I went back in and carried on with the abortion procedure.

My heart breaks just thinking about my baby. I felt totally numb to society after leaving that abortion clinic. I could not believe that the baby that I had carried with me for 14 weeks was gone. I cried for days and nights about aborting my baby. I had to leave my house whenever my mom turned on a vacuum cleaner. It was not fair, why me?

Why did I get pregnant, and why did I have to abort my baby? It did not make sense to me! My boyfriend did not even go with me to the abortion clinic, he made me face that abortion alone, and I hated him at the time for that.

This was another red flag; we really must consult the Lord about our relationship decisions. Parents it is imperative that you teach your children about good and bad relationships as this can ultimately impact their lives forever. I just want to encourage anyone who has ever gone through an abortion with regrets to allow God to wash your heart, while forgiving yourself as well as all others who played a role in that life altering decision. We ultimately make the choice to carry that act out, even when we ourselves feel as though we were pressured into what at time is considered a resolution.

Today, I know that rebellion is an option. Rebellion in this case is the boldness to ignore the pressure of getting an abortion and face the reality of the pregnancy that came with engaging in unprotected sexual intercourse. We must stop allowing fear to be lord over our mind while governing our thoughts. Proverbs 23:7 the first part of the scripture says, *"For as he thinketh in his heart, so is he."* We ultimately will follow our most dominant thoughts, be it good or bad.

Our relationship was over, and I was completely ok with that! Even though my heart felt as though it was broken into a million of pieces from what felt like betrayal, I was willing to walk away from that relationship. When the

Lord provides us with a door of escape, it is imperative that we walk through it!

Now it was time to prepare for the prom, and I started to experience mixed emotions all over again. My now ex-boyfriend asked me to go to the prom with him, and after all the drama and hurt that I had experienced throughout the year, I had no plans to attend the prom with him. However, my spirit and flesh were not in agreement.

Stop allowing the flesh to outweigh the spirit. Galatians 5:17 NIV says, *"For the flesh desires what is contrary to the Spirit, and the Spirit what is contrary to the flesh. They are in conflict with each other, so that you are not to do whatever you want."* When you truly know what is best for you, you must walk in your best even if it means leaving others behind. Having recently gone through such a traumatic experience, all I wanted to do was move forward.

Honestly, how could I move forward, was I worth enough to move? My mind was starting to play tricks on me, and I continued to take the bait of the thoughts that were contrary to my purpose. It is like this, as soon as you give attention to the contrary thoughts, the enemy will step in and began to talk to you. Those thoughts can become hidden desires, and sometimes all it may take is someone else to give voice to that thing. Here I was face to face with pressure to choose!

I was looking for sound counsel in my prom date decision, however all I got was conversation about why I should go with my ex to the prom. Today I would tell my teenage self to trust my instincts and run. In the end, we ended up going to senior prom together and graduating from high school while keeping our relationship. Looking back, I was given another door of escape on prom night, showing me that we needed to end the relationship. Ladies and gentlemen, I would admonish you to pay attention to the red flags!

Here we were digging ourselves into a deeper hole! We were entangled into a strong soul tie. Deep down inside when I left for college, I knew that I was to break up with my boyfriend, but I could not let go. The wrong soul ties are extremely dangerous and can really alter your decision-making abilities. Sometimes we hold onto the thing that GOD is trying to shield us from, which can create a will within the will of God for your life. That is exactly what I did! I was heading down a road of destruction, until God intervened.

Proverbs 14:12 ESV says, *"There is a way that seems right to a man, but in the end it leads to death."* Just like the Apostle Paul in the bible, I had an encounter with God that ultimately changed my life forever. Paul formerly known as Saul was a persecutor of Christians. He believed that he was doing God a favor by killing the believers. On the road to Damascus, per Acts chapter 9, Saul has an encounter with Jesus which changed his name forever. This is where he met destiny! Here is where my story began, or I would dare to say changed!

Chapter 4

The Encounter

I t was the spring of 2004; I was a freshman in college. It could not be true; I only have one week left until Cheerleading tryouts and approximately 3 weeks until it is time to go home for the summer break. Pregnant, this could not be happening to me right now. Here I was, facing pregnancy again one year later after terminating my first pregnancy.

This was not a part of my plan; I had so much to do. This must be a dream; maybe I am stressed out because finals are coming up. Can you say that I was in total denial? I have been going to the gym a lot lately, and my diet has changed a lot. My thoughts were everywhere at the time. I will go to Sebastian Health Center and take a home pregnancy test just for clarity or confirmation. Then I will have the proof I needed to move forward.

Ok, now all my friends are in class and my roommate has an 8 o'clock class so I could just sneak and take the test. My roommate already took her pregnancy test and received a negative result; maybe mine will say the same thing. By 10am I had not built up the confidence to take the test because at the same time I was spotting, and I thought that maybe I should give it a few more days. Listen y'all the signs were there! Everything was pointing to my new fate of motherhood. My cramps were becoming excruciating, so I thought that I just needed to rest a little.

Ok, today is the day, my roommate has just left for class, and I will take my pregnancy test now just to prove that it is negative. So many thoughts were going through my mind at the same time. I was in a state of confusion. Finally, after building up the courage, I decided to take the pregnancy test. A few minutes later, and it was time to check the result. Oh, my goodness! No, no, no, no, no, it cannot be. Then the tears began to pour, and all I could do is cry. God please, what am I going to do? I cannot believe that it is positive. This had to be a dream. I thought that I could not get pregnant right now. My life is going great; my future is extremely bright. What am I going to tell my parents? I know that I cannot go home now. Lord please, I will be careful, I will become celibate. Just give me another chance. My pregnancy did not go away no matter how much I prayed. The reality was, ready or not, I had a little life growing on the inside of me!

After days of prayer, and nights full of tears, I decided to go to the doctor's office for an accurate reading. "Ms. Glover, I have given you four different pregnancy tests, and they have all come back positive! It is time for you to accept it, you are six weeks pregnant. Congratulations!" the nurse exclaimed! As those words begin to ring a bell in my ear, it felt as though my whole world had been shaken in a moment.

Now what? Where do I go from here? Let us take a moment to reflect as I interject! Please understand that one moment can change the very course of your life. The very act of engaging in sexual intercourse will warrant so many types of responses whether you want to hear this or not. Not only does it potentially bring about pregnancy, but it also causes your soul to tie with another person's soul. Although I stated this before in a previous chapter, even if pregnancy does not occur, there are things that are happening internally that you may not be prepared for.

Today, I would advise my teenage self and my unmarried self to wait until marriage to engage in sexual intercourse. Let us get back to my story! Who can I turn to? I am only 18 years old. I am not ready for a baby. No matter what I was thinking in the moment, or how I felt I knew that I had to have my baby. I'd already told God that if I ever became pregnant again, I would not terminate the pregnancy. It was time to get a reality check, my life would never be the same. I was officially a mom!

Let the Fun Begin

After discovering that I was pregnant, two weeks later it was time to move out of the dormitory and go home for the summer. I was terrified of going home. How are my parents going to handle my new-found parenthood? Will it be easy or tough? I am not sure how this will turn out, and honestly, I am scared. My mind was racing, and stress had definitely come for me! In the back of my mind, I knew that I was entering a season of struggle.

Arriving at Union Station, I could sense the shift in affection. My boyfriend changed his posture towards me as soon as we hit the District of Columbia. The level of affection that he had previously displayed changed in a moment's time. Here we were coming home with the biggest news of our teenage lives, and I felt totally alone. What am I going to do?

Listen, together we had come up with a plan of how we were going to raise our baby, and to my surprise the plans that we agreed to were already falling apart right before my eyes. Finally, I arrived home (to Washington DC) and I suddenly felt like a stranger! Everything that I had imagined taking place was all a lie, Jeez Louise Man! I felt like a total fool!

We arrived at his mother's house first so that I could finish his hair. It had not been more than fifteen minutes of our arrival and already everyone was angry. The very first seed of discord came from my boyfriend at the time having an altercation with his sister about the whereabouts of his comb. Looking back at the situation today, I can tell you that he totally blew the situation out of proportion. Honestly, I truly believe that the comb was still in his hair and when he went to use the bathroom it fell out of his hair into the trash can.

Now let's get back to the situation as it unfolded! Out of nowhere here comes his mother yelling and screaming, you should ask your girlfriend if she took your comb. She is probably trying to be spiteful and cause you to turn against us. I stared in amazement at the false accusation against me! Are you serious? Why would I take the comb and I am the one doing his hair? What sense does that make? After a few moments, the comb was discovered in the bathroom trash can. His mother began to proclaim, here goes the comb. I knew that she threw your comb in the trash! What? Are you serious? I had not even gone into the bathroom as of yet since we arrived. How could I have done that? Common sense did not matter at the time. Everyone blamed me, including my boyfriend/ father of my unborn baby. "I want her out of my house, she is no longer welcome here," is what his mother proclaimed! All the while the tears had begun to formulate in my eyes, I WAS COMPLETELY ALONE in the matter of minutes!

I traveled alone to my mother's house all the while knowing that I would not be accepted there either. Although I did not have a 100% surety of what was going to happen when I arrived, I did not feel good on the inside. My gut was telling me that things had taken a turn for the worst all at the same time. Sometimes we have a knowing of what is to come before it happens. The Holy Spirit is called to lead and guide us into all truth. You see, I made a phone call to my parents letting them know that the semester was over, and I was heading home for the summer, and the response that I received was to stay where I was and not to return home.

The truth of the matter was that the dorm was closing, and all students had to leave campus unless they were attending summer school. Now, I knew that no one was happy with my decision yet again to carry my pregnancy to term. That day was already full of emotions, I called my mother to tell her that I was on my way home, and she told me to stay wherever I was. "What!? I am on the bus close to your house," I explained. I was not in a place where I could just turn around. I was literally in the middle of nowhere.

And right then, I knew for sure that I was not welcomed home. I was going through a cycle, and its name was defeat. In the moments where we find ourselves going through a familiar pattern, we must decide to make a change even if the process is painful. When we change our mindset, we will change our life. Make a quality decision to be the change that you are searching for.

I choose to keep my baby. This time it did not matter what I had to endure or what everyone else thought!

I choose to embrace motherhood!

There is nowhere to turn. Did I make the right choice? Despite what it looks like, God I choose to keep my baby, and it was time to prepare for a fight. Truth be told, I had entered a season of spiritual warfare and I did not even realize it! I was literally alone, and I was not comfortable in my own mother's home. The tension was so thick, and I was surrounded by shame.

"Shame is a painful emotion caused by consciousness of guilt, shortcoming, or impropriety," according to Merriam- Webster. Why isn't he here with me, is all I could think? He is totally enjoying his summer, and I am fighting just to eat daily. You see during that time; I did not have a job or a solid plan. I was told that I was not allowed to eat anything in the house that I did not purchase! Even though I had another life growing on the inside of me, what was supposed to be a joyous occasion caused me to become a disappointment to my parents.

One day I found myself in this place of total despair, the battle was on, and I did not know how to fight to win! Are the rumors true? Girl, he is cheating on you! He is sleeping with someone that is closer than you think. He is also going around telling everyone that you were sleeping with some other guy in North Carolina, and your baby is not his. He said that you found out that you had an STD (chlamydia) and he tested negative so there was no way that your baby could be his. It is funny how things changed as soon as we changed states.

My unborn baby's father literally wanted to have a baby, he intentionally released on the inside of me, and weeks later decided that he was not ready for fatherhood! Be careful of what you agree to in the moment of an act of lust. All of heaven and all of hell are waiting for our words. The bible tells us in Proverbs 18:21 NLT, *"The tongue can bring death or life; those who love to talk will reap the consequences."*

After doing some serious research and getting a second opinion through multiple tests, I found out that my diagnosis of chlamydia was false. According to one of my doctors, a lot of pregnant women were receiving false chlamydia readings at the time, which caused many relationships to end abruptly. The father of my baby was calling me a whore and having sexual intercourse with other girls just to prove that he no longer cared about me. That was for sure an immature approach to a life altering circumstance. I was not sure of how to handle this new information that I had received. I cried a lot during that season of my life. Throwing and participating in my own pity parties became the norm for me.

GOD, can you hear me? Are you listening? I AM SO HURT; MY HEART IS BROKEN...... WHAT DID I GET MYSELF INTO? I attempted to live a normal life without any indication that things were going to be okay. I had no sign of hope! I began to stay in the room all day long only coming out when my parents were gone. I was totally alone! Looking back at that time in my life, I had partnered with loneliness. Things were getting ridiculous; I was completely ashamed!

I was not allowed to enjoy my own pregnancy. The guilt of carrying my child was unbearable. It seemed as if no one was happy for me! The cycle of defeat, a repeated cycle that I had experienced during my first pregnancy, was present again. I needed at least one person to tell me that it was okay. I needed some guidance and not to be put to shame, full of embarrassment, and experiencing emotional

41

pain. I had made my final decision despite what it looked like. I choose to keep my baby! I was in a low place then. Still reaching out to the father of my child even though I knew that he had dismissed me to others. I was looking for his acceptance and approval, knowing the truth of the matter was that I was facing pregnancy scared and alone.

Ladies I was experiencing a true void, a hole in my heart that only God could heal. I was willing to be my unborn child's father number one, even if it was just for a moment. Avoiding the feelings of rejection is not worth settling for any type of negative treatment. It is not worth losing yourself for another person's satisfaction, longing to belong, attempting to mask the pain although you are screaming on the inside.

I was in a deep state of deception and denial. I was longing for attention and affection no matter the source. Honestly, that toxic relationship was covering up the emotional pain that I needed to be healed from. The type of pain that only Gods could heal. I was having a major identity crisis! John 8:32 says, *"And ye shall know the truth, and the truth shall make you free."* I was running from the truth in my mind. The truth was that I was holding onto a forever that was never meant to be. You could not tell me that he was not my knight in shining armor, or that he was not called to be my husband. I was about to have a baby by a man that was not created for me. Never once during this relationship had a consulted the Lord for his strategy for my life. I had everything all figured out, at least I thought I did!

Proverbs 19:21 (NIV) states, *"many are the plans in a man's heart, but it is the Lord's purpose that prevails."* To be honest, he was another woman's husband, and I am another man's wife. No one really thinks in that manner but to be honest, God created one man for one woman and vice versa. God knows our ending from our beginning, and we sometimes have a way of rerouting the plan of God for our own life. Truth be told, God has a perfect plan for our lives that He has designed, however it is up to us to keep those lines of communication open with the Father through cultivating a relationship, having a consistent prayer life, and seeking His face.

The moment we choose to be the Lord over our own life, we are ultimately deciding to make our own way! There is no room on the throne of our hearts for both God and man! By doing so we cause ourselves to encounter certain trials and tribulations that we were never designed for. In my one act of disobedience of consistently engaging in sexual intercourse, I struggled through an unplanned, planned pregnancy. The reason why I call it an unplanned, planned pregnancy is because we did not go through the steps of actively preparing for a baby like married couples do, we agreed to unprotected sexual intercourse in a moment of passion and stated that we would have a baby. Before that moment there was not any discussion around having a baby. In actuality, our baby was not a mistake, no matter how short the discussion was in the moment.

Chapter 5

You Are the Father!

As the days, the weeks, and the months went by, the evidence of another life on the inside of me had become more visual. Where are you? Are you coming to see me tonight? I need your help! This pregnancy is so hard for me right now, and I feel alone. I do not want to be with you, was all I heard as he uttered those words out of his mouth. I am moving on! How can you be moving on when we are pregnant and just a few months ago I was your girl? I have been nothing but faithful to you, and now that I am pregnant you want to move on? I really could not believe my ears.

Oh, my goodness! How could he say that to me? We have become complete strangers; he does not love me anymore. By that time, I was both the CEO and the President of my own pity party. My heart was broken, and every day I felt more pain. Where will I turn? I should have stayed in North Carolina and tried to find a way to live on my own. Honestly, it appeared as though my options were lessening.

Get it together Girl!

As I feel his tiny little feet kick me, I knew that I was going to be physically alone in raising my baby. My unborn baby's father had truly left me to live this kind of life of a single parent, while he was out having a good time. I was constantly sitting in the room alone, poor without a dime, nor a plan, hiding the very life that was growing on the inside of me. "God, where are you?" I cried. "Please help me! What am I going to do? Nobody wants me. How can he leave me like this? I am scared."

Being alone with your negative thoughts is a truly scary place to be in. The one thing I can admit about being in that mental space was that I knew who to call on. Jeremiah 29:12 NIV states, *"For I know the plans I have for you,* *"declares the Lord," plans to prosper you and not harm you, plans to give you a hope and a future."* You see, right there in the midst of my mess, God was still drawing me unto Himself. What a loving Father!

The rumors are true; your boyfriend has broken up with you in front of his friends, and he is telling others that you two are no longer together behind your back. Girl, I saw him the other day, you know that he has a new girl, right? Everybody knows this except you. Word on the street is that he is telling everyone that he is sleeping with her, and that he can still have you too if he wants. In that moment, I had to make up my mind, was I going to give another person that much power over me? It was time to change my posture. Sometimes you literally must take a stand that may seem unpopular to others. The truth of the matter was that I was not married to this guy, and I did not have to stay in that fight. It did not make any sense to give up my position of authority. I had to constantly remind myself that I was not in a fairytale story; he does not want to deal with you. No matter how hard it was, I had to move on!

"Kim, believe it or not you are a mother. Your son will be here in two months, renew your mind and prepare yourself right now to become a mother." Those words absolutely changed my life as my sister uttered them to me. God had spoken to me through my sister, and even still, I was becoming angry. I was angry because the person whom I thought loved me, had just rejected me while pregnant. This newfound anger helped me to change my posture. Although my outside circumstances and environment did not change, mentally I was no longer in a place of desperation for my unborn baby's father attention.

Hidden Secrets

It was not even a week later when my life changed again, and this time it felt like all hell was breaking out in my life even more. When is your baby shower? I am not sure, I do not have any money to pay for a venue, nor do I have any family members that would throw me one. Who would I invite? I have no one to really turn to, I felt so alone. If I did not need the clothes, then I would not even have the baby shower.

To get my mind off my personal life, I decided to become an assistant cheer coach at my alma mater. Cheerleading is something that I absolutely loved, and I knew that if I could keep myself busy, I would feel much better. I had begun attending practice daily and attempting to impart cheer techniques and wisdom into this new team. I now had something positive to look forward to daily. This is pretty cool, I thought, and I could work off my baby weight at the same time. The reality was that I did not know what I was about to encounter. Suddenly, the one thing that I was looking forward to enjoying every day was taken from me. How do you coach a cheer team, build a relationship with the girls only to find out that one of them has betrayed you? My heart was torn into pieces. How can you look at me every day carrying this life on the inside of me and be committing this shameful act behind my back?

Where can I go to experience peace, a sense of self-worth? Now it all began to make sense. I understood why girls that I did not know were laughing in my face. There was laughter and jokes surrounded me, I had to find out the truth. I heard the whispers behind my back daily, however I chose to ignore it. Could it really be what I think it is? It was time to for the answer to come forth.

One day during practice her phone rang and the name behind the ringtone is titled "My Boo." As I looked at the phone my heart begins to break even more, it was true he had moved on without directly telling me. I answered her phone, and his voice was on the other end. He paused knowing that he could not keep the lie hidden.

It was her, someone that I worked closely with every day. Someone who saw me more than he did, she saw the evidence of a growing life on the inside of me. All the late nights of pretending to be so busy with work, pretending to keep me out of harm, and all the while he was cheating. So, I did what any other woman would do, I went to approach him immediately. Practice was over, and I was ready to fight.

Right then I did not care how pregnant I was, I was ready to fight! Not only are you putting my health in jeopardy, but you are putting my baby's health in jeopardy. I left practice in a hurry trying to get to his house as fast as possible. I did not care about anything else; I was furious! You are a liar, and then you were defaming my character. Everyone is looking at me like a whore, and I have never been with another man before. I could not believe what was happening. The very love that I thought I was experiencing for him immediately turned into hate. I was raging! I had no more trust in him.

Today I understand that as a believer we are to put our trust in God and not in man. Proverbs 3:5-6 reads, *"Trust in the Lord with all thine heart; and lean not unto thine own understanding. In all thy ways acknowledge him, and he shall direct thy paths."* I was wrongly focusing on him, instead of me. Learning of my ex-boyfriend cheating and telling others that my baby was not his provoked me to anger. Maybe it hurt more because the one that he was cheating with was right in front of my face. The joke was on me. There is no way that I have fallen into this trap again.

In 2003, right before prom, I terminated my pregnancy and had to carry around the guilt and shame for so long. Here it is almost two years later, and he is doing the exact same thing to me again. He told me that he loved me, he said that he was sorry, that he would never hurt me again and I believed him. Now I am truly alone, I must do what is best for my unborn baby and me. "We will be ok," I proclaimed to myself as the tears continued to fall.

Chapter 6

One Word from God Can Change Your Life

Prepare yourself to be a mother, believe it or not he is on the way. One word from God can change your entire life. My older sister told me to prepare to be a mother repeatedly. Those words resonated in my spirit for the first time when I was 8 months pregnant. I was finally starting to get excited about my newfound motherhood, and then it happened!

"Look Kim you are 19 years old and about to have a baby, you have to get out of my house." I could not believe what I was hearing, and not at that current moment! I was not in the place to leave! "I do not want a grown child in my house with a baby; let him take care of you." Wait a minute, didn't she know that he had already walked away from the situation? It was around 11pm in the middle of November. You can imagine how cold it was outside in Northeast DC. What was happening to me? I had literally become homeless in the matter of a moment. My baby was due any day, and I had no idea of where I was going to take him.

"Kim you can come here for a few days, I understand that we have not gotten along, but I do not want you to have my grandson on the streets." This was the first time that my unborn son's grandmother on his father's side had spoken to me in months. Everything was happening so fast! Tomorrow we can look for some shelters for you to stay in. Really, a shelter, I was so confused! Why was that even an option?

I cannot believe this, is all I was thinking! How could he be comfortable knowing that we are about to have a baby, and I am living in a shelter while he sleeps comfortably at home with his family. Lord please, help me! I have no where to turn. I was really living in a shelter with less than 30 days until my due date. Everywhere I turned, there was someone watching me! Uncomfortable eyes were always on me. Strangers all around me in that shelter. There is absolutely no privacy in the shelter, but if I did not stay, I would have been out on the streets.

The very next day, I found myself at a new shelter in southeast DC, Catholic Charities. Living in that shelter was the first time that I had ever been on that side of DC. The southside was extremely different from uptown. I was extremely uncomfortable there and at the end of the week, I had to find somewhere else to stay. "Girl, you can stay with me. However, it is not enough space here. If you agree, I know another family that will take you in!" Instead of being in a season of nesting, I was literally bouncing from shelter to shelter! I was in a place where I had to draw on all that I knew about Father God. What I heard was that

Kimberly Glover

God was the kind of God that would never leave you nor forsake you, so I had to pull on that!

Chapter 7

I Will Never Leave You nor Forsake You

Even when mother or father forsake you, God always provides a ram in the bush. "I know that you do not know us, but my family and I would like for you to come and live with us." I could not believe it! The family that took me in did not even know me and were still willing to let me come into their home. I was both scared and grateful. The one downfall that I had was that this family lived all the way in Laurel, what a huge change of scenery for me it was. Honestly, anything was better than the alternative which was the shelter. Even still I was totally conflicted!

Every day I traveled to DC just to be surrounded with the people who were rejecting me the most. I was still in a state of total denial, I was truly gullible! The father of my unborn baby was not at the least concerned about my whereabouts, and in my mind, I wanted to be close to him no matter what. I was in between two opinions! My thoughts were all over the place! What if I went into labor in Laurel? Who would come visit me all the way out here? So, after about 3 weeks I decided to move into a maternity home in Washington, DC. The decision to move into this home was solely based on my feelings concerning being around people that I was familiar with. My mind was totally naïve, I thought that being close to the father of my child would make him love me and even make the effort to come to visit me more. Deep down inside, I was still looking for his acceptance.

Sometimes we totally miss the blessing at hand! When I told the family that I was living with about my plan to move into another shelter, they extended the invitation for me to live with them even after my baby was born, and I declined. You see, I was totally uncomfortable with the idea of living in an unfamiliar place, even though I was being treated with so much love and respect. I was totally embarrassed about my current situation. This Christian family allowed a pregnant teenage girl to live in their house without passing judgment on her. My life was unfolding in a way that I had never expected. I was full of shame, guilt, hurt, pain, and rejection. I was falling apart and had nowhere to run. The bible says in Hebrew 4:16, *"Let us therefore come boldly to the throne of grace, that we may obtain mercy and find grace to help in time of need."* God was truly keeping me all along.

The day arrived, and it was time for me to move into the maternity home, which is really a smaller shelter or transitional house for pregnant woman. I was so full of emotions. Why was I even here, I never imagined my life unfolding like this? The only people that helped me to move into the home was my sister and brother-in-law. I was devastated! I truly did not have the support that I was searching for. The father of my unborn child once again was nowhere to be found. Within two days of living in this shelter I went into labor.

The first thing I did was ask the young lady in the house about contractions and she advised me to go straight to the hospital. Can you imagine going into labor with no one there with you, to walk you through the steps? That was my story! The same young lady told me that if I called the ambulance then they would take me to Howard University Hospital, and I said no way. I did not want any parts of HUH, my experience in the past was not anything that I would prefer to experience again. I did not have anyone on standby to call if I went into labor, so I rode four different buses to get to Washington Hospital Center.

Once I got on the third bus, I called my child's father and advised him that I was going into labor. His response almost broke my heart once again, he told me to call him back when I got to the hospital to make sure that I was in active labor. So, I hung up the phone and called his mother who told me that she would meet me there.

Full of emotions, I arrived at the hospital alone, learning that I was in active labor. I ended up having my baby with three people in the room with me. Although I had my sons' two aunts, and his father there, I was scared. I could not call the one person that I dreamed of having in my delivery room with me, my mom! Who goes through labor without their mother? I was hurt, heartbroken, angry and full of joy all at the same time. After seventeen hours of labor, I gave birth to a healthy baby boy.

Chapter 8

The Moment of Truth

In Deuteronomy Chapter 30:19 it states, *"I call heaven and earth to record this day against you, that I have set before you life and death, blessing and cursing: therefore, choose life, that both thou and thy seed may live."* After leaving the hospital, I stayed with my son's father and his family for about three weeks before returning to the maternity home. I was scared and left alone to handle a fragile baby that I did not know how to handle. He was so small, I barely wanted anyone to touch him, let alone live somewhere that was foreign to me. I was in a house full of strangers.

You see in a maternity home, you must take your baby everywhere you go, even in the bathroom with you while you showered. At the time I did not understand what was going on, however, God was building some character and strength on the inside of me. God was literally teaching me how to fight a battle without me even realizing it. My newborn baby was attached to me 24 hours a day, 7 days a week. I was still so foolish. I just wanted to be accepted, so I traveled over an hour daily in the winter just to see my sons' father, and his family in order to get out of that maternity house. Not really understanding that he needed to come visits us, I was doing all the traveling in the middle of winter with a newborn baby. Can you imagine how much work I was doing just to be around someone that really did not want to have anything to do with us? One day I began to realize that this struggle is real! I was alone, and I needed to come up with a new plan.

You have to leave!

"Ms. Glover what do you want to do with your life?" During our monthly meeting with the director of the maternity house, I was asked the question of what do I want to do with my life? So, I explained to the director that I wanted to become a pediatrician. The director then asked me, due to my current situation, how was I going to achieve this goal? I informed her of my plans to go back to school and she laughed at me. Her facial expression said it all, this director literally laughed in my face. This lady told me that it was impossible! You are 19 years old with a baby, you live in a shelter, you do not have a job, or a strong support system, and you only have one year of college.

I looked at this lady who was basically calling me a failure with tears in my eyes! I could not believe that she could be so cruel, so I simply stated that I was going back to school no matter what! One thing that I know to be true is that "WITH GOD ALL THINGS ARE POSSIBLE." Matthew 19:26 says, *"But Jesus beheld them, and said unto them, with men this impossible; but with God all things are possible."* After that meeting, I received a letter in the mailbox telling me that I had just been terminated from the program at the maternity house. The director felt as though I did not qualify to be there any longer and had to vacate the premises immediately. I could not believe my eyes, I was back to square one just from weeks prior, but this time I was homeless with a newborn baby. What am I going to do now?

I called my son's father and explained the situation and his mother asked us to come stay with them. I hesitantly accepted the request and moved in with them. It seemed as if things would be getting better, right? Wrong! Things got completely worse. This was not a good idea. Imagine just having someone's baby and being treated with such disrespect. This man literally came and went as he pleased with no regard for me or our child. I was so hurt and stressed seemingly most of the time. Even still, I was determined to handle my son with love and care. Though we lived in the same house, I was literally raising our child alone. The family attempted to get involve and help us to establish some boundaries. To no avail, I was alone.

During this time, I was on welfare, embarrassed but happy that I had some type of finances coming in. Although my son's father worked at the time, he did not contribute to anything concerning our child. I felt like I had a baby with a total stranger and was completely stuck. God where are you, was my continual heart's cry? At the same time, I was not getting along too well with my son's grandmother. No new mother wants someone else to tell them what to do with their new baby everyday all day, so that broken relationship was becoming more broken.

I was at a low point in my life and knew that I had a decision to make. So, I picked up a job at McDonalds working the graveyard shift while my son slept. I went to work, and on breaks I would go to the house and breastfeed, change him, put him back to sleep then walk back to work until 5AM. It was like I never left the house. The funny thing is that my son's father and I worked at the same company during the same hours. How was it possible for me to be a single mother? I would be in the house alone all day with my son and go to work at night.

Late in the midnight hour God will turn it around.

Sometimes all you need is a little motivation! While looking at my current reality, I knew that I had to make a change. All we seemed to do was fight, and one day the fight got physical. That day marked a change in my life. There was no way that I would allow a man to put his hands on me and I continue to stay. The fight was over preparing milk for our baby, something completely ridiculous. We had to go! I finally had the courage to ask my mother if we could stay at her house for a few days.

I began to pray for a way of escape. I was totally ready to go back to school and heading to North Carolina was literally my escape plan. As soon as you tell others your plans and aspirations get ready for a Faith Fight. Needless to say, I drafted up a plan, found a roommate and my son and I moved to Greensboro, North Carolina where I re-enrolled into North Carolina Agricultural & Technical State University.

Chapter 9

The New Journey

All eyes on me! People from my freshmen year came running up to me during freshmen week. Oh, my goodness! Is that your baby? I cannot believe it; you really had a baby. Where do I start? Although some people deeply missed me, others were judging me. I am now a mom, and I must plan to stay focused and go through the process. I had a full-time course load, financial aid was in place, and I got all the classes I needed for the semester. The only thing that I was lacking was a babysitter.

In the state of North Carolina, during that time, it was extremely hard to get a daycare voucher. Knowing that I had already signed a lease and registered for my classes, the only other option for me was to take my son with me to class. God was literally ordering my steps. There was no way that I could orchestrate such an awesome plan by myself. Day one of freshmen week consisted of both new and transfer students locating their classrooms and addressing any potential needs and concerns with the advisors. I knew that the professors would be on campus during freshmen week, so I decided to use that time to introduce myself and to ask every professor for their permission with bringing my baby to class. Every professor was truly kind to me, explaining that their only issue would be if my baby cried during class time. I thought to myself that their ask was a piece of cake. I had approximately one week to put my baby on a schedule that would allow him to sleep straight through my four classes a day. To God be all the Glory, my son slept through all four of my classes every day during the first semester.

My professors were definitely heaven sent, they even added his name to the class roster, and if for some reason he was not in class with me, everyone would ask about his whereabouts. My son was six months old when he began college for the first time alongside of his mother. We continued attending North Carolina A&T SU for the remainder of that year and then journeyed back Washington DC.

Things are not always what they seem.

My experience in North Carolina changed my life. I was truly angry about some of the things that transpired, but I was determined to continue the journey. My son was now 1 ½ years old and it seemed as if we were going around the same mountains of opposition. Leaving North Carolina, I had to move in with my parents, who had expressed their negative feelings about us coming to live with them. I could not believe it; I was back in the same place. Honestly, I was homeless again. It was stated several times that I was only a visitor not a live-in member of the household. Here we go again with the same mountain of opposition. I just needed peace of mind.

One day I decided to go visit this guy that I was talking to prior to going back to North Carolina. We had hung out a couple of times and were intimate one time. This guy lived directly across the street from my parents' house. My son was sleep and my mother said it was ok for me to leave him there with her for a little while. Thinking that we were going to pick up where we had left off before I went back to school, I excitedly paid this man a visit. To my surprise when I got to his house, there were women's clothes all over the place, so I asked about his involvement. Without any hesitation he told me that he met another woman when I left, and she moved in with him.

Happy to see me, he got close to me and attempted to kiss me. I told him that I did not want to have anything to do with him because he had a girlfriend, and I would be leaving. This man then exclaimed that I was going to give him some, and I was not going anywhere. My heart began to pulsate extremely fast. Oh, my goodness! This cannot be true! I know that this man is not going to rape me. I was extremely terrified! In my mind I thought that I could not show any sign of weakness. My son was across the street sleep, and he need me. I cannot let this man kill me. I looked at the door to attempt to escape by getting up and running. This man then chased me, grabbed me, slammed me down to the couch and proceeded to pull my pants down. You can only imagine what was going through my mind at the time.

By nature, I am a fighter, there is no quit in me, and although the circumstances were very scary, I went into survival mode. While in the moment, I knew that crying was a sign of weakness, and I was not going to allow this man to have his way with me without putting up a fight. My immediate thoughts during this scuffle were that he was going to rape me and then kill me. I literally saw my life flash before my eyes knowing that this was not the end of my story. I was only about 21 years old, and my son needed me. In a desperate attempt to escape the grips of this ex-marine, I formulated a quick plan in my mind.

I began to survey the room, while fighting to see what my options were. I mentally thought about grabbing a weapon and using it on him, and at the same time, I thought about his physical strength and that my actions would backfire on me. Right in the middle of being attacked sexually God was providing me with a way of escape. I had previously ignored my uncomfortable feelings of anxiety about going to this man's house all alone. I reasoned that I'd been around him before and no harm had come to me, so I would not have to worry at all.

As I recall being in that moment, I believe that God was helping me to navigate through a new plan of escape. You see, this man lived in an old apartment building that had about 6 bolt locks on the door including a chain. The door of escape was challenging. There were bars on the windows, and he lived on the top floor, so it was impossible to jump out of a window. Remember I was in survival mode, I have never encountered a man of this type of strength! This man was able to hold me down with one hand and force his way with another hand. I was very strategic in how I got out of this apartment. How come no one heard my cries for help, did I even scream for help? I don't even know if I screamed for help! I honestly understand the thought process of a victim today.

With each time I broke free from his grip on the couch I ran to the door, knowing that he was chasing me, I strategically unlocked one of the bolt locks at a time. Honestly, I do not even think that he knew what I was doing as he was too busy trying to consistently penetrate me. The truth is that I was gaining my freedom with each lock becoming unlocked.

Rape is a form of imprisonment, it can literally cause your body to become numb, and your mind to be in bondage to not only the attacker, but to the spirit of fear. I had made up my mind in that moment that not only was I going to be a survivor, but I was more than a conqueror. I was truly an overcomer, and I was going to one day tell my story. Fear could not win; I was born to fight, and my Bible tells me that I always win.

Woman, girl, sister, daughter I declare right now in the name of Jesus be loosed and be made whole from the spirit of fear! My sister be free from the very memories of the attack that you've encountered. Choose to be a victor and no longer a victim, escape the grips of defeat! Allow shame to be loosed from your mind! Woman be thou made whole in the name of JESUS! Even as I recall this traumatic event, I remember thanking God that I was able to escape his apartment. I made it to see another day, and if you are reading this, then so did you!

Fear can really have a voice in your life if you allow it. If you want something to grow, you must feed it. Likewise, if you want something to be weakened and eventually die, you must refuse to nurture it. Mark 4:14-15 says, *"The sower soweth the word. And these are they by the wayside, where the word is sown; but when they have heard, Satan cometh immediately, and taketh away the word that was sown in their hearts."* This represents the way in which a person receives or perceives a thing. When we as people who have been a victim of assault recall the events of that night, we tend to filter our entire life around that event if we are not free from that bondage. Fear begins to run rapid in our mind causing everything to be told and heard from a victim's mindset.

I recall being extra careful about everywhere I went not knowing if someone was waiting to assault me again. After months of living a defeated lifestyle, I decided to be the change that I was so desperately looking for. I again enrolled into school, this time it was The University of the District of Columbia. I attempted to put my past behind me, all of which failed at the time. I consistently filtered every man that I encountered through a victim mindset. I went through a season in my life where I wanted to date but was afraid of how it would end.

Thinking back on this season, I was full of rage, I could not trust any man. Going on dates were challenging in the beginning because I had not released the past hurt. I went on an amazing date with this man, he treated me like such a queen but at the end of the night he decided to go home to pick up something before taking me home.

I went into a panic, here it goes again, why am I here? This man literally begged me to become sexually involved with him and fear gripped me, I explained to him several times that I did not want to engage in sexual intercourse with him, he never stopped asking. I was in a valley of decisions! He did not want to leave the house until he had his way. This man told me that if I did not let him have his way, then he would not take me home. I was literally trapped!

I eventually allowed him to have his way, feeling like there was no escape, and I cried the entire time. As the tears continued to fall, this man did not care that he had pressured me into engaging in an act that I did not want to be a part of, and afterwards he took me home. The drive home was long and terrifying. I was in a dangerous place, I now hated men!

This pattern was being repeated way too often for me, and I eventually cried out to the Lord. I was convinced that all men only wanted sex from me, and I hated them for that! In my anger I changed my position, and I took the upper hand at least I thought I did. I began to use every man I encountered for whatever I wanted from him without engaging in sexual intercourse. Sexual intercourse was not a desire of mine, but I knew it was for them, so I used it against them without delivering. No one was every going to hurt me again! I was not going to allow another man to penetrate me at my own expense and it was not even my desire.

One day, out of nowhere, my heart's desires changed. I was looking for God! I desired to know God for myself. The truth of the matter was that God was literally drawing me unto Himself even though I thought that it was my own idea. The latter part of Romans 2:4 says, *"not knowing that the goodness of God leadeth thee to repentance?"* My heart was literally crying out to God, and I had come into a place of repentance!

Chapter 10

The Rebirth of My Spirit

God, I need you! Can you hear me? My life is in shambles, and I know that You alone can change it! A light bulb went off in my mind! If I want something different, I must do something different. When Sunday came, I was in search of a church. Every week, I would get my son dressed and we would go from church to church looking for a perfect fit for us. Some days we would walk in the church and sit down for approximately 10 minutes, then walk back out immediately. I was not spiritual at the time, but I knew when something did not feel right, and we would run out of the doors. John 16:13 (KJV) says, *"howbeit when he, the Spirit of truth, is come, he will guide you into all truth: for he shall not speak of himself; but whatsoever he shall hear, that shall he speak, and he will shew you things to come."*

I was convinced that the Holy Spirit was guiding me through the process. Although I was not spiritually mature at the time, I had received Jesus as my Lord and Savior at a young age. I would never forget the day that I found my church home. My little sister was a security guard for DCPS and had to work overtime on Sundays at Lucy D. Slowe

Elementary school. Knowing that I was in high pursuit of God, looking for a church home, she asked me to come visit her at work. My sister explained to me that they were having church in the school that she was stationed at. You see to the naked eye it appeared as though I was just going to visit my sister, right? Wrong! God was totally drawing me unto Himself.

God is so strategic! All the while, it was God alone who was ordering my steps. Psalm 37:23 (KJV) says, *"the steps of a good man are ordered by the Lord: and he delighted in his way."* Once I got to the school, I sat in the sanctuary of Victory Christian Ministries International DC (VCMI –DC) and listened to the message. This message hit home, the Pastor was preaching on walking in love. I had never heard of this before! Walking in love, what was that? Since I was a first-time visitor, I was given a CD to take home. Excitement had taken over me so much that, on my 40-minute walk home I listened to the CD. Something was changing in my heart from that one word. The following week I found myself getting up extremely early to walk back to the school where they were having church. I was really enjoying this new profound teaching. The message was extremely powerful yet again. I did not mind walking back to my mother's house to and from service at all. You see, I was searching for God, and my spirit was being fed like never before.

Finally, after three weeks of visiting, I joined the church, and two weeks after that my mother told me that my son and I had to leave her house yet again. This time I found something called hope. Hope and I became good friends. The Bible states in Hebrews 11:1 KJV, *"Now faith is the substance of things hoped for, the evidence of things not seen."* A few months prior, I had worked for a temporary agency that contracted with Care First Blue Cross Blue Shield in Washington, DC. The reason I left the job initially was because I had enrolled in college courses and was unable to work and attend classes at the same time. I understood that I needed finances however, I was not scared of being without at all. Honestly faith and hoped had consumed me.

Being threatened with homelessness no longer moved me! One word from God can change your entire life. I was consistently going to church, hearing the word, and applying it to my life, so the thought of moving out gave me the courage to be bold and to exercise my faith. The word of God became my resource, to be quite honest, it had been my only resource. Studying the bible became my lifestyle. Romans 4:17 KJV was my favorite scripture, *"(As it is written, I have made thee a father of many nations,) before him whom he believed, even God, who quickeneth the dead, and calleth those things which be not as though they were."* I had hidden this word deep down inside of my heart. Calling those things that be not as though they were became my signature. I had learned that no problem I could ever be faced with was too big for my God. It did not matter the circumstance; I know that God is for me.

Moving forward, I began to search for an apartment. Remember, I did not have a job at the time and that was not going to stop me. My faith was in action! Could

I receive what I was truly believing God for? I knew for sure that if I allowed God to be my source and my only source, then He would provide for us. All I had was the word of God hidden in my heart that I began to activate. You see, the way to activate your faith is by calling those things that be not as though they were by speaking it into existence. The mouth is a powerful weapon! Your words have creative power or destructive power, and the choice is yours.

I decided to use my words to create what I wanted and needed! I had nothing to lose and everything to gain! Joshua 1:8 KJV says, *"this book of the law shall not depart out of thy mouth; but thou shalt meditate therein day and night, that thou mayest observe to do according to all that is written therein: for then thou shalt make thy way prosperous, and then thou shalt have good success."* To meditate on the word both day and night requires a posture of discipline, having your mind totally fixed on the promise of God. The word was producing in my life, you see, time was of the essence, and we needed a home. Every day I would drop my son off at daycare and then ride the bus around for hours looking for an apartment in the city.

After approximately 3 weeks my search was over! I got instantly approved to move into Wingate Apartments in southwest DC. I was extremely excited! Now that I have found a place to call home, the next step was to get a job. That same day that I got approved for the apartment, I called the Temp Agency in order to gain employment. Immediately I learned that CareFirst BlueCross BlueShield had requested that I come back to work for them. The very next day I returned to work. Things took a sudden turn in my life all in one day it seemed. The truth is that God has already written and prepared every day of our life, and it is up to us as believers to seek His face, find out the plan, and walk in it. Nothing just happens, God literally makes every crooked place straight in our lives if we dare to believe Him while calling Him into remembrance of His word.

The word of God was alive and active in our life. My son Isaiah and I resided in southwest DC for approximately three years before our life yet again took another turn. We were yet again faced with another challenge. The psalmist says late in the midnight hour God will turn it around. Throughout our stay at Wingate Apartments my son and I experienced miraculous things happening for us month after month. We had learned how to rely on God for everything, and although the journey was challenging, God had never left us. I once again through prayer had decided to go back to school and this time my desire was to attend Howard University.

Let me interject right here, I wanted to go to a university where I could fulfill my dream of becoming a collegiate cheerleader, and a school that was well known, so I began to search the website and begin my admissions process. During this time, my son was about three years old. There were many things that I desired to do as a college student that I had not achieved yet, so I was on a mission to accomplish every goal. This part of my life was called my faith pursuit! Howard University is known for academic success, and the admissions criteria is extremely rigorous.

Here is a little bit of my background on my academic journey in order to provide you with some more color. While attending North Carolina A&T State University, I was placed on academic probation because my grades had slipped below a 2.0 GPA. When I left North Carolina and returned to DC, I got a conditional acceptance into UDC on a promise to keep my grades above a 2.0 GPA which I had managed to do, and here I was attempting to get accepted into Howard University. One thing that I know for certain is that you need a sure word from God in order to get some extraordinary results.

The bible tells us in Hebrews 11:6 KJV, *"But without faith it is impossible to please him: for he that cometh to God must believe that he is, and that he is a rewarder of them that diligently seek him."* People that knew my academic history thought that I was foolish for trying to achieve what appeared to be an unattainable goal. Another thing that I am fully convinced of is that one word from God can change your life, and if we would dare to believe Him even for something that seems impossible, we dare to receive some impossible looking results. These types of results are what I refer to as a BUT GOD moment. I define a BUT God moment as a moment in which a person attains results that only the favor of God can give you. This is a place where you dare to believe God for the extraordinary despite what it looks like, the naysayers are not able to move you from this place of believing for extraordinary results. These results come from exercising your faith while standing on the word of God until you receive exactly what it is that you are believing God for.

Now back to the story of my journey through higher education. I remember going to registrar's office in order to obtain my transcripts and informing the registrar that I was preparing to transfer to Howard University. The administrator working at the registrar's office told me that I would never get accepted into HU with my kind of grades. I often wonder what type of interview process applicants go through when they apply for positions in academic institutions. It's like encountering some of the administrators and faculty can become so discouraging at times. Is there any compassion and encouragement for students who are attempting to do better than their present circumstance?

I literally had to choose to ignore her comments and attempt to discourage me. So, I did what I knew to do, I began to call those things that be not as though they were according to Romans 4:17. After receiving my transcript from UDC, I knew that I had to once again create an academic portfolio and apply to Howard University. If I was going to attend HU, I had to do something radical. Howard University was known for its academics, often called by many students, the black Harvard University, I could not afford to apply into the university the normal way. I could not mail in my application and transcript because if I did, it would get denied. I knew that if I wanted something different, I had to do something different. So, I decided to go to the admissions office myself and hand in my application.

Initially, when I walked into the Admissions office, I knew that I looked foolish! The very first woman that I encountered told me the usual, you must apply online, and we don't take hand delivered applications. You see, I was very aware of the admissions process, but I also knew that my situation was unique. Someone needed to hear my story, they needed to see my determination to succeed. So, I walked out of the admissions office determined to make it into the university. I began to pace back in forth searching for answers to my next step within. What I was doing was consulting with the Holy Spirit. John 16:13 KJV says, *"Howbeit when he, the Spirit of truth, is come, he will guide you into all truth: for he shall not speak of himself; but whatsoever he hear, that shall he speak and he will shew you things to come."*

A few minutes later I found myself talking to a nice woman in the hallway about some obstacles that I had overcome and my desire to attend Howard University. The Lord was literally setting me up for this encounter that would answer my prayers. During my encounter with that woman, she informed me that she was an admissions representative, insert praise dance!!!!!! Not only was she an admissions representative but she revealed to me that she in fact made the final decision on who actually got accepted into the university and that I would receive my letter of acceptance in about one week. To God be the Glory!

God literally favored me, just because it appeared that I was not going to get accepted into the university, did not mean that I was not. One word from God can change your life. We truly are to walk by faith and not by sight. My faith in God's ability to grant me the desire of my heart to attend Howard University literally superseded the fact that my grade point average was below the required admissions guidelines.

Chapter 11

We Walk by Faith and Not by Sight

Accurately to Roman 4:16 amplified version, *"Therefore, [inheriting] the promise depends entirely on faith, [that is, confident trust in the unseen God], in order that it may be given as an act of grace [His unmerited favor and mercy], so that the promise will be [legally] guaranteed to all the descendants [of Abraham], not only for those [Jewish believers] who keep the law, but also for those [Gentile believers] who share the faith of Abraham, who is the [spiritual] father of us all."* Just by meditating on this scripture alone, I know that I have been changed. Through faith, I could on purpose tap into an unseen realm. I found a new reality, one that was outside of the seen realm, outside of the five senses. No longer would I allow my natural circumstances to dictate my future.

You see, I had begun to see in a way that I never thought was possible. Seeing through the eyes of my heart, which was with the spirit of God literally ordering my steps. What the world told me was impossible for me to obtain, God told me something contrary. God's word told me that all things are possible to those who believe. Matthew 19:26 KJV, *"But Jesus beheld them, and said unto them, with men this is impossible; but with God all things are possible.*" I was defying the odds in every area of my life, time and time again. Nothing or no one could stop me but me. It no longer mattered about what it looked like, if I could believe for it then I would walk in it, and the situation would change for me.

One year later I found myself creating a vision board for one of my classes and presenting it to my peers first, and then a group of students from Baltimore City Public Schools who were on a college tour. The unique thing about this vision board presentation is that just about everything that I placed on my vision board had come to pass. I remember it like it was yesterday. I thought everything was going great during that time until I got back to work only to find out that my assignment was up. This had all happened in the same day. I had been working for this agency for approximately 3 years and had recently changed supervisors, now three months later I was losing my job. Determined to stand on the word of God, I continued to matriculate at Howard University for the remainder of the year.

My son and I were in survival mode, month after month, we were believing God for the finances to pay our bills, to eat, and to travel back and forth to school. During the same time, we had allowed one of my classmates in need of a place to live for the summer to stay with us. Every day I was praying that eviction would not come near us. Coming home from class every day became a celebration when we stuck our keys through the lock, and the door opened once again. I can remember seeing about five apartments being evicted at one time, and one of my neighbors had the same living room furniture as me. I rushed off the bus and into the apartment building, and once again we were spared. Psalm 91:7 (KJV) which states, *"A thousand shall fall at thy side, and ten thousand at thy right hand; but it shall not come nigh thee,"* was my daily prayer. It was the word of God that was protecting us from all harm. I was calling those things that be not as though they were daily. Approximately 3 weeks later, we had received an eviction notice, the Marshalls literally gave us a 14-hour notice to vacate the premises. It was around 7pm on a Thursday night when we received a notice underneath the door to vacate the apartment by the very next morning. There was nothing that I could do about it, so I got my five-year-old son dressed and we rented a UHAUL truck with the little money we had left.

Eviction day had come, and my son and I were completely alone. There was no one there to help us move. We lived in a high-rise apartment building and the only elevator that was big enough to contain furniture in it was the freight elevator on the opposite side of the building. Standing at 5 feet 1 ½ inches tall, approximately 145 pounds at the time, and my 5-year-old child, we managed to pack up everything in our apartment and move it to the truck before the Marshall's arrived. I was so angry! I could not believe that no one would help us to move out. Looking back at all the things that I had acquired; it was hard to once again be forced to give away everything that I had worked so hard for. We went from the Salvation Army to the thrift store giving away all our belongings including furniture. My heart was torn, I was back in the same place once again, experiencing another eviction where I was coming out with nothing. Through it all I knew that God had not left us. I was reminded of Deuteronomy 31:6 (KJV) which states, *"Be strong and of a good courage, fear not, nor be afraid of them: for the LORD thy God, he it is that doth go with thee; he will not fail thee, nor forsake thee."* My life yet again took another turn!

The Turn Around

Sitting in the room on the floor in my friend's apartment, I heard one of Marvin Sapp's song play in my mind. The words, "He has his hands on you" play repeatedly in my mind, as my son sat in my arms and smiled. In a matter of a moment everything was taken from us and here it was my son still had joy. I began to apologize to my five-year-old son for having to sleep on the floor, and his response melted my heart, He said, "Mommy I don't mind as long as I am with you." God was literally with us, he was protecting my son's heart, while covering us in the blood of Jesus.

After two months had gone by, we packed up our minivan and moved to Baltimore City. The journey to Baltimore was a little shaky but it absolutely changed our lives. My son and I found ourselves residing with my sister and brother-in-law for about two years. Sleeping on the floor daily, trying to find a way to survive, it literally felt like all hell was breaking out in my life, and all the while God was taking us through a process. Looking back, I can see that God was keeping us! Each day we were trusting God with our life, and each day God supplied our need. God was showing himself strong in our lives, taking care of us daily. According to Philippians 4:19, (Amplified) which says, *"And my God will liberally supply (fill until full) your every need according to His riches in glory in Christ Jesus."* I definitely learned in this season that no matter what it looked like, God never left us. In fact, God was really preparing us for our next season! We were going from faith to faith!

Chapter 12

Weeping May Endure for the Night, but Joy Cometh in the Morning!

After months and weeks of being unemployed, submitting application to company after company, I heard a message from Dr. Creflo Dollar about how-to walk-in victory. The part of the message that stood out for me, was when he talked about getting into a situation where he needed to hear from God immediately. We will all experience opposition in life! Sometimes in the midst of a defining moment we have to be quiet!

The bible tells us in **Proverbs 18:21 KJV,** *"Death and life are in the power of the tongue: and they that love it shall eat the fruit thereof."* If we are not careful to think first, and to be slow to speak, we can employ the wrong kingdom to move on our behalf. Dr. Dollar was experiencing a pause moment! His pause moment required him to hear clearly from God. In the message, Dr. Dollar was instructed to put on his walking shoes and to take a walk-in effort to not only get his heart right, but he needed to hear clearly from the Spirit of God.

In that moment it dawned on me that it was time for me to put on my walking shoes, I was in need of a breakthrough, and the only way my breakthrough was going to manifest was if I heard clearly from the Holy Spirit and followed the precise instructions that I was given. I had made a quality decision to shift my mindset and to seek God intently, knowing that I was not going to get any results in my own strength. **Matthew 6:33 NKJV**, *"But seek ye first the kingdom of God, and his righteousness; and all these things shall be added unto you."* Seeking God became the norm for me; I wanted to know what God's thoughts and plans were for me in the midst of every situation.

I knew that I had work experience, so it was time to get my job God's way. One morning the Lord had instructed me to walk my son to school as we did daily, but this time I was instructed to wear business attire and to bring tennis shoes with me. So, I followed the instructions that I was given! After I left the elementary school, I once again consulted the Lord for my next step. Seeking God is a continuous process, so after reaching the next destination I continued to inquire until the journey was reached.

The Holy Spirit led me to Johns Hopkins Eastern campus, from there I rode a free shuttle to the Johns Hopkins Hospital. When I got to Johns Hopkins I began to light up, I knew that I was where I was supposed to be, so I began to take territory. For me, taking territory meant praying over the ground, speaking into the atmosphere, and declaring the promise. I was supposed to work for Johns Hopkins in that season of my life, although every job that I had applied to up to that point had rejected me. I knew that all the promises of God are yes and amen, so I began to speak it into existence!

After about two hours of praying, decreeing and declaring, I got back onto the shuttle heading back to Eastern Campus so I could take my 1 hour walk back home. While I was sitting on the shuttle at Johns Hopkins Hospital, a students began to ask me if I just left an interview, I told her no, and she then proceeded to provide me with the necessary information to connect me with Johns Hopkins human resources department. This student advised me of how challenging it was to get into Johns Hopkins as a student and employee, however, the quickest way of entry would be to seek employment through a staffing agency. Again, I was in the right place at the right time, talking to the right person.

I took the lead that was given to me and was immediately employed by a staffing agency whose client was Johns Hopkins Hospital. For months I worked as a contractor as an Admission Representative Assistant prior to the assignment ending. That position was a total blessing, the admission's rep told me to apply to attend the university if I was interested and she would admit me. Can you imagine how much excitement was running through me, knowing that one of my desires at the time was to attend medical school at JHU.

The fulfillment of one season

Moving forward my vision was beginning to change yet again, I was eager to fulfil the will of God for my life in that current season. Graduating from college was a major accomplishment that I had yet to fulfill. The upcoming academic year was approaching, and I needed to enroll in classes. During that summer I was still traveling back and forth to Howard University to attend summer classes that I had yet to pay for. I was desperate to graduate! I knew that I was going to get dropped from classes and yet I still attended every session.

At the end of the summer session, I knew that attending Howard for the following semester was not in my best interest due to the commute, my academic progress, and the tuition. After seeking the face of the Lord again, I was instructed to enroll into Morgan State University as a senior, but not as a graduating senior. Admissions into Morgan State University was extremely challenging, my GPA once again was less than a 2.0 and the admissions office did not want to accept me into the university.

To be honest, I was not qualified! Nevertheless, I was determined to matriculate from MSU with a Bachelor of Science. You see this time; I had consulted the Lord on where exactly he wanted me to attend college. As believers we are to inquire of the Lord for everything, not just in the challenging situations. **Psalm 37:23 KJV** says, *"The steps of a good man are ordered by the Lord, And He delights in his way."*

Walking in total submission to the Lord was crucial to my success.

When I made up my mind to walk in obedience, the fight was on. The fight was concerning inheriting the promise. This time I even consulted the Lord about what major to pursue before I assumed that Biology was going to be my major. I received a peace about pursuing a degree in Psychology, so I headed over to the Psychology department for advisement. My encounter with the Dean of Psychology was extremely disturbing. This lady not only discouraged me from continuing with the admission process into the university, but she told me that I would never make it into her rigorous program. She went on to explain to me that the Psychology Department took a scientific approach, and because of my previous failure in the Biology Department at Howard University, I could never complete the program at MSU.

Fighting to hold back the tears until I left her presence, I was distraught! It was the moment of truth for me, what was I going to believe? My flesh was telling me to no longer pursue my admissions to MSU, but my spirit was exclaiming that with God all things are possible. The bible clearly states in Deuteronomy 30:19, "*I call heaven and earth to record this day against you, that I have set before you life and death, blessings and cursing: therefore, choose life that both thou and thy seed may live*". Lord, I choose life!

Weeping may endure for a night!

Weeping may endure for the night be joy cometh in the morning! It was after my weeklong plead with the admissions office that I was admitted conditionally into the university with the promise of maintaining a 2.0 GPA. You see, God had already given me the green light to pursue admissions to the university, I was now the determining factor. One word from God can change your life if you choose to believe it. There will almost always be a no from someone when God is calling you to go higher. Remember this, with man nothing is possible, but with God all things are possible to those that will believe. Needless to say, I graduated from Morgan State University in 2015 with an overall GPA of 3.3. Now the same Dean of Psychology who once told me that I would never graduate from her rigorous program conferred my degree. As I proceeded to walk across the stage and shake her hand, I wanted to remind her of the negative words that she spoke into my life the first day that I was pursuing admissions into the Psychology program.

On graduation day, I thought about all the other young men and women that just needed a chance to correct a wrong; those who just needed a second chance to make a better impression. I thought about every hopeless young lady that should have said no but said yes to one night of passion that changed her life forever. I thought about all the other single moms that used their circumstance as an excuse to stay stuck and defeated. I thought about everyone who told me that I had ruined my life when I became a teen mom. I thought about the director of the maternity home in Washington, DC, who told me that I was dreaming, and that I could never finish college. I thought about all the naysayers that said that this day would never come for me. I thought about every young lady that carried a dream and aborted the very vision because of a lack of support. I thought about all the mothers that could not see how accomplishing her goals was possible and could become her reality. I thought about the excuses of not having a babysitter, could be perceived as a lack of support that a parent think that they need in order to become successful. On May 16, 2015, I knew that I had broken through the cycle of defeat in my life. My testimony represented so much more than just graduating from college, it represents hope, change, progress, faith, love, overcoming, in high pursuit of, it represented victory by being empowered to win!

How do I know that I have been changed you asked? I knew that I had been changed when God became the focus of my life. It was in the uncomfortable, impossible looking times that I had chosen the blessing. It was in every decision to do it God's way. Although we are not perfect, we can daily strive to be pleasing in the eyes of the Father. I had decided to choose life no matter how hard it may seem. When I faced a pivotal point in my life, I made a quality decision to trust God, knowing that He alone had my best interest at heart.

I knew I was changed the moment other people's perception of me no longer tainted my heart. Now, determined to finish whatever I started by defying the odds and ignoring the negative reports, everything had become possible for me. No longer was I partnering up with the enemy and settling for pity parties, while inviting others to join me, I had changed lords! Jesus Christ is my Lord and Savior, and His word is truth. Applying Romans 12:2 daily, the amplified version, *"And do not be conformed to this world [any longer with its superficial values and customs], but be transformed and progressively changed [as you mature spiritually] by the renewing of your mind [focusing on godly values and ethical attitudes], so that you may prove [for yourselves] what the will of God is, that which is good and acceptable and perfect [in His plan and purpose for you]."*

I literally changed my mind! I began to see what was possible for me, with the understanding that my past or even present circumstance could no longer dictate what would become my reality. I began setting a greater goal and vision for myself to walk in a new reality. Overcoming and dominating impossible looking situations by faith was a must! I had to show my son something different. Poverty was no longer an option, the only thing that I wanted to expose my son to, was that with faith all things are possible. Faith takes what it has a right to! My son needed to see what can become a reality with faith, patience, perseverance, and some applied pressure. Having a vision was just the beginning! If I really wanted to change my reality, I had to take what belonged to me.

I quickly learned that taking what belonged to me was a process that required diligence. Consistency, perseverance and faith was my key to success! Defeat was no longer an option. I had to go through a trial period of staying consistent and keeping my eyes on the goal. One of the lessons I learned in that season was that things are not always as they appear! You literally must push past the obstacles and press into your promise. Delay is not a denial! We can truly have everything that we set our minds to, because with faith and patience, we will no doubt inherit the promise!